HAPPY HOUSEPLANTS

How to Grow and Maintain Your Indoor Plants

by
Violet Rutherford

JBG PRODUCTIONS
Los Angeles
Printed in the United States

JBG PRODUCTIONS
960 North Larrabee
Suite 323
Los Angeles, California 90069

TABLE OF CONTENTS

THE HOUSEPLANT

A Brief History of Houseplants

Throughout history man has added natural beauty to his home by growing plants indoors. Early civilizations helped ease the dreariness of long, harsh winters by surrounding themselves with the lush, colorful foliage and flowers of the houseplant. Additionally, humans long ago realized that many plants offered medicinal or culinary benefits.

By the beginning of the 1800s, explorers from all over the world began exchanging plants, and rare and exotic species from the Orient, Africa and Europe began to appear in the Americas. Soon, over 5,000 different species of plants were being grown inside of homes all around the world. As the 19th century rolled around, the Victorian English became the leading plant lovers in the world, cultivating different types of plants in greenhouses, parlors, bedchambers, sunning rooms, conservatories, libraries . . . everywhere and anywhere!

In the 1980s we tend to use plants as accents to our home decor rather than as the dominating objects in any one room. We hang plants from the ceiling, place plants in windows, highlight a corner of a room with a lovely arrangement of plants . . . anything that will make our homes seem fresh, alive and beautiful!

What is a Houseplant?

The ancestors of the houseplant are those plants which grow in shady, tropical forests. Plants in this type of environment enjoy wet, humid conditions, seasonal changes in temperature, and soil which is very rich in nutrients.

Since we cannot always duplicate this tropical environment in our homes, I like to say that the houseplant of today is like a wild horse who must be tamed for work on the ranch. Like the wild horse, the houseplant must learn to adapt to a different way of life, to domesticity.

Fortunately for you and I, the key characteristic which each houseplant shares is its ability to adapt to the environment of the average home. Every plant does have its own needs however, and as a houseplant owner, you must be aware of these special needs if your plants are to survive.

HOW TO BUY
A HOUSEPLANT

Choosing a Plant That is Right for You

Whether you are a novice buying a single houseplant for decorative purposes, or an experienced plant hobbyist purchasing many houseplants to add to your growing collection of plants, the important thing to remember is to choose a plant that is right for you.

What kind of plants do you like? Flowering plants? Foliage plants? Cacti? Do you like to prune? Do you like plants with large leaves or plants with small leaves? These are among the types of questions you should ask yourself before you buy any plant.

Another important question relates to the size of the plant. Have the place in your house where you'd like to put your new plant in mind when you go to make a purchase. This way you won't buy a plant that is too big for the space in your house, or too small to fill up such an area.

The specific location where you wish to put your plant should also help you decide what type of plant to buy. Check the lighting, temperature and humidity of the location, and only buy a plant which is suited for such an environment.

Another important consideration when buying a plant is the amount of care you are willing to give the plant. If you are a busy person who does not want to spend a lot of time caring for a plant, you should buy mature plants which are extremely adaptable to all kinds of lighting, humidity, watering and temperature conditions. For those of you who are interested in owning plants which require only minimal care, I have included a chapter entitled "Houseplants for Busy People." The plants listed in this chapter may be the wisest plants for you to purchase.

Additionally, in "The Encyclopedia of Houseplants," also included in this book, I have devised a rating system which grades individual plants on how easy they are to take care of. Look up the plant you are considering purchasing and see if the amount of care it will require matches the amount of care you are willing to give it. If you find yourself with a plant that is too difficult to care for do not let it die! Instead, trade it or give it away to someone who will be able to offer it the attention it requires. While the decisions you have to make before buying a plant may seem complicated right now, after reading through this book, you will find that picking out the perfect houseplant is an easy, fun-filled task!

What to Look for When Buying a Houseplant

Once you have decided what type of houseplant will suit your needs, it is time to find a plant dealer who will sell you a healthy plant. While everyone loves to find a bargain, it is much safer and wiser to always buy your houseplants from a reputable florist, nursery, or plant boutique. When you visit one of these plant dealers, carefully evaluate the shop's selection of plants. If the plants seem to be in good health, and the overall atmosphere is one of an attractive and well-groomed store, chances are good that the plant you buy will be very healthy and will subsequently live for a long time with proper care.

When picking out a plant, inspect it carefully for any signs of damage. Be on the lookout for brown edges on leaves or any evidence that these brown areas may have been cut away. Inspect leaves and stems for any sign of pests or diseases. If you can spot pests or some leaf damage, the plant will most likely continue to deteriorate once it is in your home. Also, look at all supporting stakes and screens and make certain that they are not concealing damaged stems, branches or trunks.

Any healthy flowering plant should have plenty of buds ready to burst open. If most of the buds have already bloomed, you should look for a less mature plant. If the new leaves of a plant you are thinking of buying have large gaps between them, there is a good possibility that excessive amounts of fertilizer have recently been applied to the plant in order to make it grow more rapidly, or that the plant has lived for too long in poor light. Avoid buying any plant in this condition.

Additionally, be sure to check for any roots growing out of the bottom of the pot. If you see roots poking out through the drainage holes this is a sign telling you that the plant has outgrown its container. If this is the case you have two choices: One, you can look for another plant, or two, you can ask the owner of the store to repot the plant into a larger container for you; in some instances there will be a slight charge for this service.

If the plant you are interested in purchasing is free of any defects, if its color looks good and it shows signs of new growth, your choice is an excellent one! Congratulate yourself and welcome the plant into its new home where it will begin a happy, healthy lifestyle under your care.

CARING FOR YOUR PLANTS

Tools

If you are serious about giving your plants the proper care which they deserve, it is important that you have some basic tools and materials at your disposal. While many gardening tasks only require tools you already own — your fingers and hands — there are certain jobs which will demand tools other than these parts of your body. Virtually everything I recommend owning can be bought inexpensively at any garden center.

To begin with, a watering can with along, narrow of the temperature in various rooms within your house (thermostats are usually inadequate since they tend to display the temperature only in one room), are both important items to own. Addtionally, if you think that the humidity level in your home might be a problem, a hygrometer — a device which records the humidity level in the air — can be a useful instrument to purchase.

I also believe that it is a good idea to have a solid countertop or table to do your work on. Since this will be the area where you will be doing your potting, pruning, grooming and other assorted and often messy tasks, the surface should be made of a material that is easy to clean.

The most basic tool every plant lover should own is a quality pair of standard pruning shears. In addition, a sharp knife often comes in handy. These two items are essential for grooming, pruning, and propagating your plants.

Various kinds and sizes of containers — both plastic and clay — are a good thing to have around for the different types of planting tasks you will be engaging in. Along with these pots, a collection of small, broken pieces of pottery is mandatory for any potting job.

A bag of all-purpose soil, along with certain additives like peat moss, compost, or ground bark is also helpful to keep handy for all of your planting needs. Additionally, liquid fertilizer and powdered rooting hormone are also essential materials for any houseplant owner.

While you may not yet understand why it is necessary to own some of these materials, don't worry! By the time you have finished this book, you will know exactly how each of these tools can help you maintain and grow happy, healthy houseplants!

Temperature

Fortunately, the majority of the houseplants being sold today have no problem adjusting to standard indoor temperatures. There are essentially three temperature ranges found in the average household: Cool (55 to 65 degrees), average (65 to 70 degrees), and warm (70 to 85 degrees).

Since a thermostat only records the temperature of the particular room it is located in, you should take a thermometer and check the temperature of the different areas where you plan to keep your plants. While most plants will adapt to any of these three temperature ranges, certain plants will grow better in particular temperatures, so it's best to check "The Encyclopedia of Houseplants" located in the back of this book to see exactly which plants will adapt best to the temperature in your home. Most plants prefer a drop of at least five degrees in the temperature at night, as this allows them to relax after a busy day of growing. The main thing to remember is to avoid putting plants through extreme changes in temperature. Plants kept near windows often have to endure much warmer temperatures during the summertime and much cooler temperatures during the wintertime. In these instances, when the weather becomes too extreme, keep a careful watch on plants in these locations and move them if they show any sign of deterioration.

Make sure that you do not place plants near air conditioning or heating ducts, fireplaces, radiators, or any areas where appliances which give off heat and moisture (i.e., a dishwasher, oven or washing machine) are located. An exception to this rule are tropical houseplants, which may enjoy a location in a sunny kitchen or bathroom, where moist heat and direct sun combine to recreate the warm, humid conditions these plants enjoy.

On this note, allow me to add that I like to keep my cool-loving plants, such as Camellias, Azaleas and certain Orchids, in rooms where bright or indirect light keep temperatures relatively lower than in other areas of my home.

Humidity

Humidity and temperature are very closely related: When air becomes warmer — either naturally or artificially — the humidity level tends to decrease quickly. This is most evident in regions where temperatures are extremely warm during the summer months, or during wintertime, when the heating unit in the household is being used.

While houseplants such as Cacti or Succulents require dry air conditions, the majority of the plants you will be growing in your home need humid conditions in order to survive. The easiest way to determine the humidity level of your home is with a hygrometer, a device that measures the moisture in the air. These are readily available at most nurseries or hardware stores.

If the air in your home tends to be on the dry side — less than a 50% level — you should try one of the following methods for increasing the humidity in the areas where you keep your plants:

Humidifiers: A cool vapor humidifier placed in an extremely dry home will not only increase the level of comfort for your plants, but for your family too! Portable humidifiers can be placed wherever needed, while a humidifier installed as a part of your central heating unit can increase the humidity level in your home by as much as 25%.

Misting: This is the easiest and least expensive way to boost the humidity level for any plant. Ferns and Orchids respond especially well to misting, but be aware that certain fuzzy-leafed plants, such as the African violet, should not be misted as spotting may result. It is best to mist in the morning with lukewarm water. Spray with a fine mist so that a cloud is created around the plant (be careful not to damage furniture or other household items that may be harmed by the falling mist).

Humidity Trays: These are another popular method for dealing with low humidity levels. Begin with a tray at least two inches in depth. Make sure the tray is waterproof, that is, one made out of such materials as metal, rubber, plastic or glazed ceramic — clay trays should be avoided for they will retain moisture and may damage any furniture they are resting on. Fill the tray with pebbles, pea gravel, perlite, vermiculite, or small rocks and add water, stopping just below the top of the pebbles.

When you place the plant's container on top of the rocks, make sure that the pot does not touch the water (which could result in root rot), and your plant will enjoy a higher level of humidity — you can check the level with a hygrometer, just make sure you take the reading close to the plant itself.

Naturally Humid Rooms: Another way to boost the humidity for a particular plant is to place the plant in such naturally humid rooms as the bathroom or the kitchen. The hot water used in these rooms generates humidity that certain moisture craving houseplants love!

Grouping Plants: If your plant desires just a little bit more humidity, grouping it together with other houseplants can give it the extra moisture it needs. Since water evaporates from any plant's leaves during the natural process known as "transpiration," the area immediately surrounding a group of plants will be naturally more humid than an area where a plant sits alone. Additionally, your plant will enjoy the company of the other plants! Just make sure to leave enough room between the plants to allow for proper air circulation.

Light

Deciding how much light your plant needs can be a very tricky decision to make. If a plant is receiving too much or too little light, it could die. In general, foliage plants need less light than flowering plants, and most houseplants enjoy plenty of partial sun or bright light rather than direct sunlight. However, these are only very general rules and they do not apply to every plant. Therefore, in order to help you make sure that your plant is getting the right amount of light, I am going to use a system which will tell you exactly how much light individual plants require. Throughout this book, and especially in "The Encyclopedia of Houseplants," you will see me use the following categories to describe lighting conditions:

Direct Sun
Partial Sun
Bright Light
Filtered Light
Shade

Here are the definitions for each category:

Direct Sun: This type of sun is normally found in areas with south facing windows. Sunlight pours in for at least five hours a day. Only a few plants can tolerate this much light, mainly Cacti and certain Succulents. However, many sun loving plants, if given some shade protection and lots of water, will survive in these locations.

Partial Sun: This includes locations which have windows facing either east or west, and which thus receive direct sun for less than five hours per day. Flowering houseplants especially enjoy these locations, but you must provide adequate shade protection in west facing windows during the summertime.

Bright Light: These are areas which receive a great deal of light through the reflection of sunlight off of ceilings and walls, but which do not receive any direct sun. The majority of the foliage plants you will buy enjoy this type of light.

Filtered Light: This refers to light which shines through either an overhang or trees and bushes outside of the window, or through blinds or curtains inside of the window. Normally, an area approximately five to ten feet away from a window which receives direct sun for a portion of the day may fit into this category. While only a few flowering plants can tolerate this fairly low lighting condition, many foliage plants can adapt very easily to this type of atmosphere.

Shade: This type of light can be found in interior rooms which receive no light from windows. Most houseplants cannot survive in such conditions without the aid of artificial lighting.

When choosing a lighting condition for your plant, the most important thing to remember is that both the intensity of the light and the length of time the light hits that particular spot in your house are the two factors which will affect your plant the most.

You must also be aware that the growth of your plant will depend on the seasonal increases and decreases in light intensity. Therefore, during the summer, when the intensity of light and heat is at its strongest, plants will grow faster and will need more moisture and fertilizer than during winter months when the light is less intense.

The portion of the country that you live in also affects the amount and intensity of light your plants take in. If you live in a high elevation, your plants will receive a higher intensity of light than someone who lives at sea level. Snow, smoke, haze, fog, screens, porches, shrubs growing outside of windows . . . there are many things that can influence the type of light your plants will get in your home.

Because there are so many different factors which

alter the amount and type of light your plants are taking in, it is extremely important to be on the lookout for signs that your plant is receiving too much, or too little light. Too much light will cause a plant to wilt and its beautiful green leaves to fade. Too little light forces a plant to drop many of its leaves and to grow unusually thin, long leaves.

Another important lighting tip concerns plants which are kept near a window. Always be sure to turn these plants every now and then or else the plant will begin to grow in the direction of the window — where its source of light is coming from. Additionally, be aware that windows can magnify the heat from the sun, and that plants kept near a window during summertime are susceptible to leaf burn.

If the space you choose for your plant does not offer it a sufficient amount of light, you can either boost the amount of light it is receiving through the use of artificial light — a fluorescent light fixture is the most efficient way to do this — or simply give the plant less fertilizer, thus discouraging it from growing at a rate which would require a type of light you cannot offer it.

Water

While quite possibly the easiest of all plant caring techniques to master, improper watering is the most common way the average houseplant owner destroys his own plants. Usually the plant's death is a result of overwatering — not underwatering — the plant. When you overwater, the excess amount of water combines with improper drainage and forces the roots of the plant to rest in water, resulting in root rot.

How much water should you give your plants? Well, this depends on many individual factors, including light, temperature, humidity, type of container, and, of course, the type of plant in question.

In general, plants with a large amount of flowering buds, or those with many young leaves, will need more water than plants that are either in full bloom or that contain leaves which are all roughly the same size and color. Plants with a large leaf surface, such as Ferns or Wandering Jews, require more water than plants without much foliage, and plants with softer leaves are thirstier than those with waxy or succulent leaves. Additionally, in the winter, plants generally require less water than in the summer.

These rules do not, however, apply to every plant, so it's important that you learn how to tell when a plant needs water. There are many techniques which have been devised for this task, including fancy, high-priced electronic meters which, when placed into the soil, beep or flash if it's too dry. However, these devices are not always accurate, so I recommend using your own eyes and fingers to judge whether or not your plant needs water.

If your plant is drooping or wilting, chances are good that it could use some water. Do not, however, rely on this so-called "sight method" everytime, for a plant can only survive a few drooping periods during its lifetime. The oldest and most proven method of judging a plant's need for water is the simple touch test. With your index finger, feel the soil down to about one inch deep. If the soil feels dry, add water; if the soil is moist, do not water and check the plant again in the next day or two.

Be aware that there are certain plants which thrive in more moist conditions than this however. For instance, Ferns, Gardenias, and African Violets prefer the soil to be slightly moist at all times. Meanwhile, Philodendrons, Coelus, and Monstera prefer the soil to be dry on the surface, but moist underneath. For your specific plant, check "The Encyclopedia of Houseplants" section of this book for its individual watering needs.

When you decide that your plant does need water, try to do it during the morning hours and avoid using water that is either too hot or too cold. Also, make sure that you give all of your plants a thorough soaking. If you simply water the surface of the soil, the roots will not receive an adequate amount of water. The important thing to remember about watering plants is not the amount of water that you give them, but the frequency with which you water them. Finally, always be sure to remove any standing water from the saucer kept beneath the container.

A wonderful trick that I have learned over the years is that hanging plants and plants on slabs of tree fern love to have their pots occasionally soaked in water. During the warmer months of the year, about once a month, put the pot in a sink of water until the water rises to just above the rim of the container. When the bubbles stop rising to the surface of the water, remove the pot, let drain, and return it to its regular place. Again, be sure to empty the saucer of any standing water. The period just following one of these soakings is also a good time to fertilize your plant.

Lastly, if your household is equipped with soft water, you should water your plants with either bottled water or the tap water from an outdoor faucet. A little known but important fact is that soft water contains high amounts of sodium which can prove to be harmful to your plants. On the other side of the coin, if you live in a region of the country where the soil is very alkaline and the water is unusually hard, you will have great difficulty trying to grow such acid loving plants as Azaleas and Camellias. The result are plants whose leaves turn yellow. Try using fertilizers that contain an acid reaction, or adding peat moss. If, however, your plant's foliage remains yellow despite these remedies, place one ounce of iron sulfate into every two gallons of water and use this solution every two weeks until the foliage becomes green again. Thereafter, keep a watchful eye on your plants in case the problem returns.

Containers

Often overlooked or bought for decorative reasons only, the type of container you place your plant in actually has a large effect on how much water your plant will require. When looking to buy a container for your plant, there are a few general rules you should try to follow.

First, try to choose a container that has a drainage hole. This will make watering your plant a much easier task, and more importantly it will reduce the risk of overwatering.

Second, buy a container that is suited for your individual plant's size. If the container is too small, you'll find yourself spending more money on another container in the near future when the plant outgrows its small home. If the container is too big, not only will you have wasted money on an extra large pot, but the plant will be unable to obtain all of the water from the soil, and the excess moisture may eventually lead to root rot.

Lastly, when buying a container for your plant, make sure you also get a drip saucer to place underneath the pot. This will save your furniture and floors from becoming water marked. There are many different types of containers on the market today. Listed below are the most popular kinds, along with some hints and suggestions which I think you'll find most helpful.

Red Clay Pots: I believe that red clay pots are the best containers you can buy to grow your plants in. Why? Because clay pots are fairly inexpensive, most nurseries or garden centers carry them in all different shapes and sizes, and their reddish-brown color usually blends in well with most home decors. Also important is the fact that clay pots are porous, which as far as your plants are concerned, means that moisture is absorbed easily and that air circulation is very good.

Because of their excellent absorption of moisture, plants kept in red clay pots will generally require more frequent waterings than plants kept in other types of containers. However, if you soak your newly bought clay pot in water for several hours before planting anything inside of it, you will lessen this condition somewhat. Regardless, make sure that you check plants kept in this type of container often for signs of dryness.

Another advantage of clay pots is that they will actually warn you if you are giving your plant too much fertilizer, or if the water you are giving your plant is too hard. If a white film builds up on the outside of the pot, then there is a problem with either the fertilization or the water.

Finally, if you wish to reuse a clay pot, make sure that you scrub it thoroughly in warm water. Better yet, sanitize it by placing the pot in an oven at 180 degrees for thirty minutes, or soak the pot in a solution made up of one part household bleach and ten parts water.

Plastic Pots: This type of container also has many advantages. Since plastic is a lightweight material, these pots are both easy to handle and clean. Plastic containers which are clear make it easy for you to keep an eye on your plant's root system. Like clay pots, plastic pots are available at almost any garden store, and come not only in different shapes and sizes, but also in various colors.

The only problem with plastic pots is that — unlike clay pots — they are nonporous. Thus, the soil inside of a plastic container will retain moisture longer than soil in a clay pot will. This means that plants grown in plastic pots will not have to be watered as often as those in clay pots.

The lesson to be learned here is that if you use a plastic pot, you must be very careful to avoid overwatering. It is probably a good idea to use these types of pots only for plants which require a large amount of moisture. In all cases, make sure that soil drainage is excellent.

Glazed Pottery: Glazed pottery is normally made of clay, but contains a ceramic glaze which causes it to become nonporous. The same warnings that apply to plastic pots come into play here. If you fall in love with a certain glazed pot, it would be much wiser to use it as a jardiniere — an ornamental pot which holds a smaller pot containing a houseplant.

Metal Containers: These should also only be used as a jardiniere. Corrosion, tarnishing and lack of a proper drainage hole are the most common problems associated with metal containers. If you find that you just have to use a metal pot, be sure to line it with a thick plastic material (especially if the pot is copper, which can kill a plant whose roots it comes in contact with), and treat it as you would any other nonporous container, such as plastic or glazed ceramic.

No matter what kind of pot you decide to buy, if it has a drainage hole be sure to place a saucer beneath it to prevent unwanted water stains on your floors and furniture. Saucers should be waterproof and nonporous, and you should always empty saucers when they become filled with water in order to prevent any damage to not only your plant, but to the surface below as well.

Once again, pots without proper drainage should only be used for decorative purposes. Since the soil retains all of the water you pour into a pot lacking a drainage hole, overwatering can become a significant problem. If you must use such a pot, never add more water than an amount equal to one-fourth of the total volume of the container. Additionally, allow the top half of the soil to dry out in between waterings.

Fertilizer

When a plant grows outdoors in the ground, the amount of nourishment available to it is almost endless. However, when a plant is being grown indoors in a pot, it only has a certain amount of soil at its disposal. Consequently, a houseplant only has a limited quantity of nutrients available for its own use. Therefore, it is your job to make sure that your plant is getting the nutrients necessary for its health and growth by adding fertilizer to its soil.

Fertilizers are sold in many different forms, including liquids, powders, water soluble pellets, time-release pellets, dry tablets, and sticks which you place into the soil.

While tablets, sticks, and capsules are the easiest to use — you simply put them on or under the soil — I prefer to use liquid fertilizers because of their flexibility. With liquid fertilizers you have the ability to dilute the liquid with water in order to get just the right amount of fertilizer you need for any particular plant.

When you first buy a houseplant, there is usually no need to fertilize it for approximately three months. Additionally, plants kept in containers only need to be fertilized when they are in a period of active growth. When applying fertilizer, always make sure that the soil is nice and moist.

During periods of active growth, you should fertilize every two weeks. If the fertilizer you purchase has been formulated for use once a month, simply feed your plant half of the recommended amount every two weeks. This is a much more effective and safer method of fertilization. Always follow the instructions on the label of your particular fertilizer carefully and be sure to keep track of the dates on which you apply the fertilizer.

Plants should be in perfect health before you fertilize. Never fertilize any plant that is infested with pests or suffering from any type of disease — wait until infected or infested plants are completely healthy before applying any fertilizer. Additionally, dormant plants should never be fertilized. This is especially true during winter months, when most plants like to hibernate. Wait until you see signs of new growth when the spring comes.

If you have been feeding a plant on a regular basis, and the plant isn't growing, chances are good that the plant is either in a dormant state or is in poor health. If this is the case, refrain from fertilizing until your plant recovers or enters an active growth stage.

Be especially careful not to give your plants too much fertilizer. Fallen, brown leaves, or a chalky film on the outside of a clay pot may indicate overfertilization. If you do happen to apply too much fertilizer, don't panic! Simply water the plant until the water comes out ofthe drainage hole, wait until the plant has completely drained, and repeat this process two or three more times. This common method is known as "leaching."

Soil Mix

I believe that along with light and water, correct potting soil is the most important element needed for growing happy, healthy houseplants. The crucial thingt to remember about soil is that it should be well-draining, while at the same time be able to retain enough nutrients and moisture to ensure proper plant growth.

The easiest way to make sure that your plant has the correct soil is to buy the pre-packaged, standard soil mix for houseplants available at most nurseries or garden supply stores. Be certain that the soil has been sterilized to prevent the spread of any pests or diseases.

If you'd rather mix your own soil, all you have to do is combine equal amounts of washed sand, garden loam or topsoil, and peat moss. For every two quarts of this mix, add one half cup of charcoal and one half cup of perlite. You can buy all of these ingredients at any nursery or garden supply store.

Once you have mixed the ingredients together, you must sterilize the soil in order to destroy any pests or diseases which may be living inside of the mix. To sterilize, dampen the mixed soil and place it in a two to four inch baking pan. Place the pan in a two hundred degree oven, and bake for about two hours. Remove the now sterilized soil and let air, uncovered, indoors, for a few days. Then simply store the fresh mix in plastic garbage bags. You should be aware that when baking the soil, an unpleasant odor may result. Fortunately, this odor is not long lasting.

For Begonias, African Violets, and Philodendrons, a soil mix which has a high humus content and is more acid may be necessary. Simply combine equal amounts of peat moss, sand, topsoil, and leaf mold. Then follow the directions for sterilization mentioned above. This type of soil can also be bought in a pre-packaged form at most nurseries under the name of "African violet mix."

A large amount of Bromeliads and Orchids are known as "epiphytes" — plants which grow on trees or rocks. For these types of plants, a lighter mix is often needed. A potting mix made up of one part clean, washed sand, one part fir bark, and one part sphagnum moss, will work very well.

Finally, Cacti and Succulents often need type of soil that contains a lower organic matter, and is neutral in pH. These desert plants will enjoy a soil made up of one part sand, one part garden soil, one half part crushed brick or clay pot, and one half part decayed leaf mold. Once again, be sure to sterilize according to the instructions given above.

Potting Techniques

Transplanting is essential for maintaining healthy, happy houseplants. In addition, repotting offers many excellent benefits for plants, including a roomier living area and fresh soil.

One of the most basic warning signs that your plant may need to be repotted is when its roots begin growing out of its container's drainage hole. Also, many times growers ship plants to nurseries in soil that is made up of very light perlite or vermiculite. This type of soil will need to be changed after your plant has adjusted to its new surroundings, usually about a week or two after you have purchased the plant. Additionally, if your plant's foliage looks too dense for its pot to handle, or if the plant is growing at an abnormally slow rate, it may need to be transplanted.

The first thing you need when replanting a houseplant is a clean pot. As I mentioned earlier in the book, scrub used containers in warm, soapy water and rinse thoroughly. Then, soak the pot in a solution made up of one part household bleach and ten parts water, and if the container is made of clay, you can also place it in an oven at 180 degrees for thirty minutes. Any porous containers (clay pots for example), should be soaked in water immediately prior to repotting, so as to keep the plant and its soil nice and moist.

Choose a pot that is neither too large nor too small for your plant. In general the new container should be no larger than two inches in diameter than the old pot. An exception to this rule is when you are transplanting an extremely large plant — one whose container is in excess of ten inches — in which case the new pot should be at least two inches wider. Another general rule to follow when potting a plant is to use a container whose diameter is equal to one-third to one-half the height of the plant. Be aware that this rule does not hold true for tall, slender plants.

Since planting tends to be a very messy process, I always cover my work area with newspaper to make cleaning up a much easier task. You should work at a fast pace in order to minimize the shock to the plant, and if you happen to be interrupted because of some emergency, make sure you cover the rootball of the exposed plant with a damp towel.

To transplant, first knock the rootball out of its present container by holding the stem and soil surface with one hand while turning the pot over with your other hand. Knock the rim of the pot against a hard surface — this should loosen the rootball enough so that it comes out in one piece.

If the rootball refuses to budge after repeated strikings, place a sharp knife between the container and the rootball, run it around the perimeter of the pot a few times, and turn the plant upside down — the rootball should come out easily.

Next, place a piece of an old clay pot, or a curved stone, over the container's drainage hole. This will prevent any of the fresh soil from pouring out during the planting process. Be sure, however, that the piece you use does not completely cover up the hole; it should resemble a bridge rather than a cork.

Begin adding the new soil until you come to the point where, when you place the rootball into the pot, its top reaches approximately one half inch beneath the rim of the container. In large pots, leave at least a full inch.

Once you have your rootball in the correct position — centered about one half inch below the top of the pot — fill in the sides with the fresh soil, occasionally tapping the container on a hard surface to settle the soil. Continue doing this until the soil is even with the top of the rootball. Then, lightly cover the point where the stem and the rootball meet, leaving the stem totally exposed. Smooth the surface lightly with your fingertips, and then water your repotted plant well.

A newly planted houseplant sometimes experiences trauma when it is first moved from its old home, so don't panic. Unless the plant is a sun loving plant, keep it in a cool spot for a few days. If the plant begins to wilt, do not give it water until the soil is completely dry to the touch. Misting the plant may help to give it some life. Finally, never fertilize a newly planted houseplant for approximately three months.

Propagation

Propagation is the method by which you can create new plants from old ones. It is by far the most rewarding and least expensive way to maintain a healthy plant habit. Along with saving you money, propagation offers you the thoroughly enjoyable experience of watching your plant grow from a stem or leaf into a lush, mature houseplant! You can grow new plants through the use of stem cuttings, leaf cuttings, plantlets, and a popular technique known as "division."

Stem Cuttings: This is the most popular form of propagation. Simply cut the top few inches off of a stem, and slice it just above a leafbud. Remove the lower leaves, and dip the stem into a rooting hormone — available at almost any garden center or nursery.

Take the freshly dipped stem and plant it in a rooting medium that is coarse and which holds water extremely well. A combination of equal amounts of sand and peat moss is an excellent rooting medium, as are vermiculite, perlite or milled sphagnum moss. Since the rooting medium should be moist when propagating cuttings, I prefer to use plastic pots, which are nonporous and retain moisture better than clay and other porous containers — a fact you undoubtely remember from the earlier chapter on containers!

When the cutting begins to grow, gently remove it from the rooting medium and check its root length. If the roots are between one quarter of an inch and one inch, it is time to place the cutting into standard potting soil.

Leaf Cuttings: Plants such as African Violets, Rex begonias, and certain Philodendrons are able to propagate themselves from a leaf cutting. Simply cut off a leaf and proceed as you would with a stem cutting. For Poinsettias or Geraniums, cut the leaf and rub the sliced end with alcohol. Let the cutting dry in a cool, dark area, and, once again, continue as you would with a stem cutting.

Plantlets: A plantlet is the tiny plant that develops as a sort of appendage on a full grown plant. Tolmieas, Chlorophytums, and Fernsall have plantlets. For rooting a plantlet, place the appendage, while it is still attached to the mother plant, in a pot containing moist potting soil. A paper clip may be necessary to place over the plantlet in order to keep it in contact with the potting soil. Keep the soil moist and when the plantlet begins to form its own roots, simply cut the mother plant's stem off as close to the plantlet as possible.

Division: This is the technique by which you divide a plant — roots, foliage, and all — into two or more individual plants. Plants such as Ferns, Spider plants, Bromeliads, African Violets and certain Succulents often have many stems at their base which make them excellent beneficiaries of division.

To divide a plant, start by removing the mother plant from its pot. Then, clear the potting soil away from its roots, and with a sharp knife, cut through the center of the rootball, making sure that you leave part of the main root and stem systems on each side of the divided rootball. Plant each division immediately and give them plenty of water. Place the plants out of direct sunlight and keep the soil and root systems moist until they take root and gain a healthy appearance. Then move your two new plants to their proper location and resume normal caring techniques.

Pinching and Pruning

There often comes a time when, because of the height of your ceiling or the space available on a table or shelf, you will need to maintain a certain size and shape for your plant. The easiest and safest way to keep a plant at a particular size is through careful pinching and pruning.

Pinching forces a plant to become more full and bushier, while pruning helps to reshape a plant that may have grown too large and unwieldy for its surroundings. The only tools you will need for such jobs are your thumb and forefinger, and a pair of pruning shears and a sharp knife for the occasional tougher job.

Pinching is an excellent way to keep such heavy foliage plants as a Wandering Jew or a Tolmiea and soft-stemmed plants like Wax and Angel-wing Begonias or Geraniums, in robust, well-groomed shape. Additionally, certain plants grown from a seed or cutting, for instance a Coleus, will simply grow straight up unless you pinch out the tip as soon as the plant has a few leaves. This will force dormant buds to burst into active growth, and with continued pinching in the weeks to come, your sparse Coleus plant will turn into a healthy, bushy houseplant.

Pinching is actually a very simple operation. All you have to do is take your thumb and forefinger, and delicately pinch off the top of stems or branches, just above the leaves. By doing so, you force the growth of the plant to change direction, thus forming new branches in any desired location.

Be aware that not all plants require pinching; plants that have only one growing stem — Palms, for example — cannot tolerate such grooming. Also, be sure that when you do pinch a stem on a heavy foliage plant, that the stem you pinch has several sets of leaves attached to it. Pruning is a slightly more complicated method that cannot only shape a plant in an attractive manner, but also breathe new life into it. An infected or diseased plant can regain healthy form via pruning, while flowering plants can be urged to bloom with this common technique. Flowering plants such as Fuchsia, Gardenia, Miniature rose, and Flowering maple will have a more attractive shape and will blossom more lavishly as a result of the pruning care you offer it.

For pruning, scissors or small pruning shears will often be necessary. There are essentially two ways you can prune. One method is to cut off a stem at its point of origin, thus encouraging new growth in the other stems or at the base of the plant. The other technique is to cut the stem off just above a leaf, thus forcing new growths at the pruning point and ultimately resulting in a much denser plant.

Choose the method that will give your plant the look you desire it to have.

Grooming

Routine grooming is something every plant owner should do with extreme regularity. In addition to the various methods outlined in the previous pages, you should keep the leaves of your plants, especially larger plants, free of dust. Gently wipe off each leaf with a damp cloth or sponge. I often use a mild solution formed of water and dishwashing soap to help me clean my plants.

If you happen to clean a plant infested with bugs or that is suffering from a disease, make sure you don't use the same rag when you go to clean your other plants, or else you risk spreading the ailment throughout your healthy plant collection.

As I previously mentioned, many plants, with the exception of those with fuzzy leaves, also enjoy a shower with lukewarm water about once a month during summer months. Additionally, always be on the lookout for dead leaves, branches, pests and other diseases. A simple examination every few days will help to keep all of your plants healthier and happier.

WHY DID MY PLANT DIE?

Warning Signals

Plants rarely die of natural causes. Surprised? Well, the number one cause of death among plants is simply improper care. That's right, you and I are a plant's greatest enemy. On the other hand, only you and I can save a plant from dying an early death.

There are many warning signs your houseplant will give off if it is receiving improper care. By making sure you check up on your plants every few days, you can cure many problems with simple measures before the problem grows into something that can eventually kill your plant. Here are a number of warning signs and what to do when you spot them:

Yellowing Leaves: These are often caused by either too little or too much light, or too little or too much fertilizer. High evening temperatures or overwatering can also contribute to yellowing leaves. Carefully watch your watering techniques and check to see if the plant needs fertilizing. Many times yellowing leaves are the result of a deficiency in nitrogen, a problem that can be corrected by spraying the leaves with a foliar fertilizer.

Wilting: This is often the result of a poor location, too much sun or high temperatures, or too much or too little water. Move the wilted plant to another location and watch how much water you give to it.

Spindly Growth: This simply means that your plant is not receiving enough light. Pinch the excess growth and gradually move the plant to a sunnier location.

Browning Leaves: When leaf margins and tips turn brown, they are most likely suffering from too much or not enough water, too much sun or high temperatures, dryness of air, or over-fertilization. Try and check each of these possible symptoms to pinpoint the problem. Salt damage can also cause leaves to turn brown. To cure your plant of excess salt, simply "leach" out the salt by flushing the plant with water two or three times — remember to wait until the plant has completely drained in between each flushing.

Dry and Brittle Leaves: This is generally the result of too little water or air that is too dry. Watch your watering habits carefully and try to raise the humidity level around the plant by misting or using one of the other techniques which I outlined earlier in this book.

Refusal to Bloom: A plant that normally flowers but is not blooming may have many things wrong with it. High evening temperatures and lack of light are two of the most common problems. A well-lighted, cooler spot is one solution, or simply move the plant to a cooler location at night.

Spotted Leaves: Leaves which become spotted usually do so as a result of sloppy watering habits. When you spill cold water on the leaves of certain sensitive plants, they may become spotted. Try to be more careful while watering, and remember to use lukewarm water.

Using Chemicals

If you discover that your plant is under seige by either pests or some type of a disease, you have two options: You can either remove the infested or infected portion of the plant by hand and/or a careful washing, or you can try to control the pest or disease through the use of chemicals.

I always recommend a thorough washing before you do anything drastic. If, however, your plant has reached an advanced stage of deterioration, a pesticide or fungicide may be the only thing left that can save it. Therefore, I believe that it is permissible to use chemical controls — but only as A LAST RESORT!

The danger of using these sprays is that the chemicals you put on the plant to get rid of its pest or disease may actually be worse than what is damaging the plant! If you do use a spray of one type or another, be sure to follow the directions very carefully, and make sure that the chemical is not going to seriously damage your plant. Ferns and other sensitive plants are especially endangered by many types of chemicals, so be careful. Once again, READ THE LABEL!

Pests

Aphids: These tiny insects have green, soft bodies and like to congregate on buds, stems, and leaves — basically wherever there is any new plant growth. Aphids do not usually have wings. They tend to cause deformities in the leaves of the plant they are attacking, and they are known to give off a material known as honeydew, which will often eventually turn into sooty mold — also harmful to your plant (see below).

To get rid of Aphids, wash the plant off with a hose, and if the problem still exists, use a combination of insecticidal soap (available at most garden centers) and water from the hose. If you find that you must use a plant insect spray, find one which contains orthene, resmethrin, or pyrethrins. Be sure to follow the directions closely.

Cyclamen Mites: These insects appear in the form of a fine dusty film, usually onthe underside of the infested plant's leaves. They are commonly found on Cyclamens, African Violets, and Geraniums. Cyclamen Mites can cause deformed leaves, flower buds, and stems.

To get rid of Cyclamen Mites, first destroy any infected leaves. Since these pests are difficult to get rid of, washing the plant will probably not be a good enough solution. Try buying an insecticide containing either disulfoton (disyston) ordicofol (kelthane) and follow the directions carefully. If the plant is so badly infected that neither of these chemicals can kill them, destroy the infested plant before the pests spread to your other houseplants.

Leaf Miners: These pests make themselves noticed by the small tunnels — usually white or tan squiggly lines — they create on the leaves of your plant. Chrysanthemums, Cinerarias, Codiaeum, and Columnea are the favorite targets of Leaf Miners.

Fortunately, Leaf Miners are fairly easy to spot and destroy. Simply cut off any leaves which show signs of infestation, and give the plant a complete washing. If the pest has done considerable damage to the plant, use a systemic insecticide which contains meta-sysox-R or orthene.

Fungus Gnats: Fungus Gnats are very small, dark, slender insects who fly around infested plants. Often they may be spotted moving across the plant's foliage and soil, and occasionally they may be seen on the windows surrounding the infested plant.

If simply washing the infested plant thoroughly does not work, the most effective way to get rid of Fungus Gnats is to spray with an insect spray containing diazinon. Follow directions carefully.

Mealybugs: These are white cottony or waxy insects which are large enough to be seen with the naked eye, but who tend to form on leaf stems, the undersides of the leaves, and in pockets where light is not able to illuminate them. The insects are known to group together, which causes something that looks like tiny cotton balls. Mealybugs cause distorted growth and secrete a substance which makes the leaves of the infested plant seem unusually shiny and sticky. Their secretions can lead to sooty mold (see below).

To control Mealybugs, simply touch the insects with a cotton ball dipped in rubbing alcohol, which kills them instantly. For more extreme cases, use an insect spray containing orthene or resmethrin and oil, or move the plant outdoors and use a more potent mix containing malathion, diazinon.

Scale Insects: These pests are found on stems, nodes and leaves. Sometimes they may look like white, cottony clumps, while other times they may appear as brown or reddish hard-shelled bumps. They normally give off a honeydew material which results in shiny, sticky leaves, often leading to sooty mold (see below).

To control these pests, carefully remove them with your fingernail or a small knife by using a gentle scraping action. Washing the plant with a mixture of water from a hose and insecticidal soap will also destroy these pests. Touching them with cotton dipped in denatured alcohol or using an insect spray containing orthene or resmethrin and oil is also a method of ridding your plant of these pests — follow the directions carefully, especially for sensitive plants.

Spider Mites: These insects are so small that they can only be recognized by the webbing that they leave on the foliage of infested plants. Another way to spot Spider Mites is to place a piece of white paper under a leaf of the infested plant and tap the leaf with your finger. If moving red, green, or yellow specks appear on the paper, your plant is infested with Spider Mites. Spider Mites thrive in dry, warm weather. Since Spider Mites are extemely contagious to your other plants, you must isolate any infected plant immediately. Then wash off the plant with water from a hose, and if necessary, a mixture of water and insecticidal soap. Any pest spray which contains orthene, resmethrin and oil, or pyrethrins is effective in killing Spider Mites. Cool temperatures and increased humidity conditions can help to discourage these pests from returning.

White Flies: White Flies are small white insects with wings which flutter around the plant. Because of the white, waxy powder which forms on their bodies, White Flies attacking a plant often resemble a white cloud. Infested leaves often turn a pale color, and may look exceptionally shiny and sticky because of the honeydew left by the White Flies (once again, a condition which may lead to sooty mold — see below).

Washing with a hose, or using water and insecticidal soap should cure your plant of infestation by White Flies. For more severe cases, use an insect spray containing either orthene, malathion, resmethrin, or diazinon. Be aware that you'll need to spray at least once a week for approximately one month to completely get rid of these pests.

Diseases

Crown or Stem Rot: This disease is usually the result of overwatering or lack of proper drainage in the container. Plants suffering from this type of rot tend to turn brown or wilt quickly. Many times the base of the plant's stem or trunk will become soft and discolored. Usually there is not much hope for a plant that has reached the severe stages of this condition, however, there are a few things you may like to try in a heroic effort to save the plant.

First, try cutting out the area of the plant most severly damaged and apply a fungicide to the remaining portion. For plants which are not too badly infected, try to repot the plant in a potting soil that offers fast and easy drainage. Set it slightly higher in the soil than you would normally do, and be sure to remove any of the old soil off of the roots of the plant.

Botrytis Grey Mold: This type of mold appears as brown spots on the leaves, and often times, the stems of the plant. When they show up on flowers, the spots may be either purple, tan, white, brown, or even the same color as that of the flower. When the humidity level is high, infected areas of the plant may be covered with a fuzzy brown or grey growth.

To get rid of this mold, first remove all diseased portions of the plant, especially infected flowers. Move the plant to a warmer location with good air circulation and avoid spilling water on the plant's foliage and flowers.

Leaf Spot: This disease shows up as brown spots on leaves; in severe instances, the entire leaf may turn brown. Dracaena and Dieffenbachia are the most common plants infected with the disease. Too much heat, high humidity or lack of proper ventilation are the most common causes of Leaf Spot.

To get rid of Leaf Spot, first cut off all infected portions of the plant. If the plant is badly infected, you many want to apply a fungicide containing benomyl or benlate to prevent the disease from coming back. Make sure you make the proper environmental adjustments after treating the disease.

Powdery Mildew: This is the most common houseplant disease. Powdery Mildew can attack leaves, plant buds, or stems, and appears as a white or gray powder. In extreme instances, leaves may curl up or become distorted. Too much water and not enough air are the most common causes of Powdery Mildew. Begonias and other soft-leaved plants are highly susceptible to the disease. To get rid of Powdery Mildew, first destroy all infected areas of the plant, and move the plant to an area in your house which will provide adequate air circulation. Watch your watering techniques very carefully. If the mildew returns, use a fungicide containing benomyl or benlate.

Root Rot: Root Rot is a common disease that is caused by overwatering. Yellowing, wilted leaves are an early sign of root rot.

The first step to take when attempting to cure your plant of Root Rot is to make sure that the plant's soil is draining properly. Also check to see if the saucer beneath the container is holding water — a condition which produces what is commonly known as "wet feet." Always remove any standing water from your saucers.

If you find that your plant is indeed infected with Root Rot, remove it from the soil, wash off any soil clinging to its roots, cut off any damaged roots, and repot the plant in fresh potting soil. During the following month try watering the soil with a mixture of benomyl or benlate and water. Be aware that cases of extreme root rot are often difficult to cure.

Sooty Mold: This type of mold is the result of secretions from such houseplant pests as Aphids, Scale, White Flies, or Mealybugs. The mold appears as a coating of soot on the surface of the plant's leaves.

The first thing you must do when you discover Sooty Mold is to rid the plant of any pests which are producing the honeydew that ultimately turns into Sooty Mold. Next, wipe the leaves off with a damp cloth. If you successfully rid the plant of the pests it is infected with, your plant should survive with no problem.

HAVING FUN WITH PLANTS!

Children of all ages are always fascinated by watching things grow. A wonderful way to provide educational fun is to help them grow their own plants — right from fruits and vegetables you have in your refrigerator!

Growing an Avocado

Take a ripe avocado and divide it into two halves. Remove the pit and wash it off thoroughly. Place the pit — with the round side down — in a container filled with water so that only the bottom half of the pit is in the water. Put the container in an area with partial sun. After approximately two months, roots will begin to form. When you see these roots, begin adding standard potting soil to the water in a 1:1 ratio. After two weeks of this treatment, pot the avocado plant. With some patience and a bit of luck you'll soon have a beautiful houseplant!

Growing a Pineapple

Cut off the crown of a ripe pineapple, leaving about two inches of the fruit attached, and place it in a container of sand. In approximately two weeks, roots should begin to form. When this occurs, plant the crown in moist, standard potting soil and you will soon have a beautiful Bromeliad! Do not, however, expect to enjoy fresh pineapple from your plant —unfortunately, these rarely appear.

Growing Carrots

Carrots and other root vegetables such as turnips,

beets or radishes are among the easiest items in your refrigerator to grow. All you have to do is cut off the tops of these vegetables, trim off the old leaves, and place them in water. Soon you'll have a lush patch of fresh greenery!

Growing a Sweet Potato Vine

Choose a ripe sweet potato with fairly smooth skin. Make sure that it hasn't been treated with chemicals to prevent growth (ask the produce man in your market). Place toothpicks in the sides of the potato and put them on the edge of a container filled with water so that the tapered half of the potato is in the water. Place the container in a location which receives direct sun. Roots will soon sprout and then, watch out, because they will grow and keep on growing as long as you keep the roots in water! Using pins, drape the vines around your window or let them wander around your table or countertop.

Growing a Citrus Fruit Tree

Take the largest seeds from any healthy orange, lemon or grapefruit, wash them off and soak them for twenty-four hours. Then plant them in standard potting soil — just below the top of the soil, and about an inch apart — and place the pot in an area that receives direct sun. Give them plenty of water and wait for the seeds to sprout. When they do, transplant each seedling into its own pot, add some liquid fertilizer, and in a few years you will have the fruit trees you always dreamed of owning!

HOUSEPLANTS FOR BUSY PEOPLE

Listed below are those plants that, with only a minimal amount of care, should live for years and years. The common names of the plants are given in parenthesis. Plants marked with an asterisk are included in the encyclopedia which follows this section.

Aechme fasciata (Vase plant)
Aglaonema (Chinese evergreen)
Araucaria heterophylla (Norfolk island pine) *
Bromeliad *
Cacti *
Chlorophytum (Spider plant) *
Cissus (Grape ivy)
Coleus *
Diffenbachia (Dumb cane) *
Dracaena (Cornplant) *
Ficus *
Hoya (Wax plant)
Palm *
Pelargonium (Geranium) *
Peperomia
Philodendron *
Pilea *
Plectranthus (Swedish ivy)
Saintpaulia (African violet) *
Sansevieria (Snake plant)
Spathiphyllum (Peace lily) *
Succulents *
Synogonium (Arrowhead plant)
Tolmiea (Piggyback plant) *
Tradescantia (Wandering Jew) *

AN ENCYCLOPEDIA OF HOUSEPLANTS

An Encyclopedia of Houseplants is designed to provide you with more specific information regarding the care of your individual plants. Used in conjunction with the tips and techniques outlined in the first portion of this book, the encyclopedia will help you grow and maintain happy, healthy houseplants.

While most of the categories which make up the charts on the following pages are self-explanatory, I feel it is necessary to comment on a few of them to avoid any misinterpretation or confusion.

The defintions of the light categories can be found in the earlier section on "light" under the chapter entitled, "Caring for Your Houseplants." When the suggested humidity level is "high," you may want to use one of the methods outlined in the "humidity" section for boosting humidity levels in your home.

The suggestions regarding proper fertilizing techniques should be executed under the guidelines outlined in the section on fertilizing. You should pay particular attention to the tips regarding reducing the amount of fertilizer to one half of the recommended doseage in order to feed your plant twice as often as normally suggested.

The "Care Rating" system should be interpreted as follows:

**** — Extremely easy to care for; anyone with a minimal amount of knowledge about how to care for plants should have no problem maintaining these plants.

*** — A slightly more demanding plant, however, if you've read through this book, you should be able to grow these plants without any difficulties.

** — You should not attempt to raise these plants until you have grown some of the *** plants and have mastered all of the techniques I have outlined in this book.

* — These plants are only for those of you who have complete confidence that no plant will die while under your supervision. If you feel that you are ready to become a true plant hobbiest, these plants will present quite a challenge for you, but will also bring you tremendous satisfaction when you are successful with them.

FLOWERING HOUSEPLANTS

ABUTILON

Common Names: Flowering maple, Parlor maple, Chinese bellflower.

Description: Once among the most fashionable houseplants of the Victorian era, this member of the Hollyhock family has regained its popular status in recent years. The bushy plant features maple-shaped leaves and plenty of striking flowers resembling small hollyhocks.

Temperature: 70 degrees days; 60 degrees nights.

Light: Partial sun.

Water: During spring and summer months, keep soil evenly moist. In the fall through winter months, allow the top of the soil to dry out between waterings.

Humidity: Normal level.

Pinching and Pruning: Groom often. Prune tips of branches heavily during fall and winter.

Fertilizer: Once a month.

Soil Contents: Common indoor all-purpose mix.

Propagation: Seeds and cuttings root best in spring.

Pests and Diseases: Mealybugs, Scale, Spider Mites and White Flies.

Care Rating: **

Abutilon

Begonia

BEGONIA

Common Names: Begonia.

Description: This is an extremely large and diverse group of plants. Some Begonias are enjoyed for their beautiful foliage, while others are loved for their vibrant flowers.

Temperature: 65 degrees.

Light: Bright light.

Water: Allow the top of the soil to dry out between waterings. Empty saucers immediately.

Humidity: High level.

Pinching and Pruning: Pinch back new plants to prevent leggy growth.

Fertilizer: Every two weeks throughout the year.

Soil Contents: African violet mix.

Propagation: Seeds, stems, cuttings and division.

Pests and Diseases: Botrytis Grey Mold.

Care Rating: ***

BROMELIAD

Common Names: Bromeliad.

Description: An exotically beautiful group of plants whose thousands of species include the pineapple.

Temperature: 70 to 75 degrees.

Light: Partial sun or bright light.

Water: Allow the top of the soil to dry out between waterings. Keep the cups of the epiphytics filled with water and change the water once a month.

Humidity: High level.

Pinching and Pruning: Remove yellow and brown leaves.

Fertilizer: Once a month during spring and summer.

Soil Contents: Epiphytic soil mix or one part clean, washed sand, one part fir bark, and one part sphagnum moss.

Propagation: Plant the "pups" or offsets in a light soil.

Pests and Diseases: Mealybugs, Scale, and Root Rot.

Care Rating: ****

Bromeliad

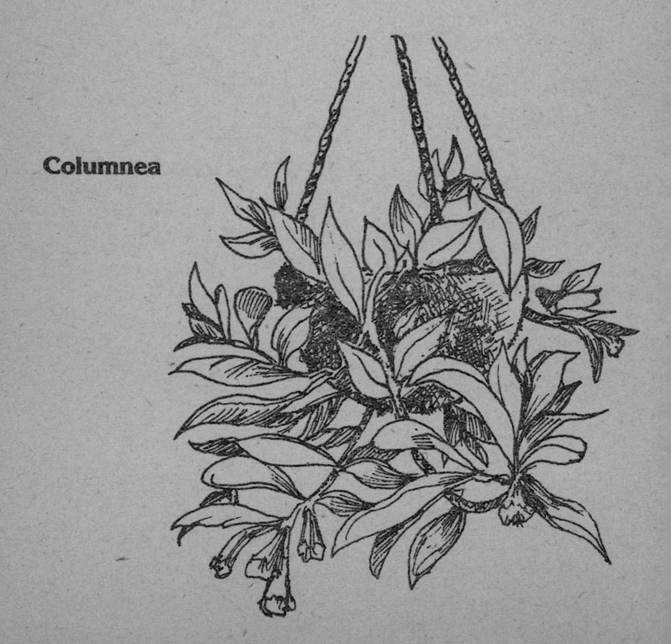

Columnea

COLUMNEA

Common Names: Norse fire plant.

Description: A trailing plant with shiny, green-purple leaves. Beautiful tubular flowers bloom in red, yellow, and orange colors.

Temperature: 70 degrees.

Light: Bright light.

Water: Keep soil moist.

Humidity: High level.

Pinching and Pruning: Prune branches and stems in spring to encourage flowering.

Fertilizer: Fertilize every two weeks except in winter.

Soil Contents: African violet mix.

Propagation: Seeds and stem cuttings.

Pests and Diseases: Aphids and Leaf Miners.

Care Rating: *

CYCLAMEN

Common Names: Shooting star, Alpine violet.

Description: Markedby heart-shaped leaves and plenty of red, lavender, white and pink flowers.

Temperature: 60 degrees.

Light: Bright light.

Water: Keep soil very moist and mist the leaves often.

Humidity: Low level.

Pinching and Pruning: None needed.

Fertilizer: Every two weeks when blooming.

Soil Contents: African violet mix.

Propagation: Seeds and tubers. For tubers, wait until blooming period ends and place tuber in a cool location and let soil stay dry. During the next summer, replant in a small container in a warmer location. Resume normal care when plant begins to grow.

Pests and Diseases: Rarely bothered.

Care Rating: *

Cyclamen

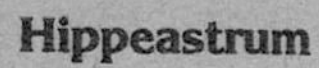

HIPPEASTRUM

Common Names: Amaryllis, Barbados lily.

Description: Known for their lovely, lily-like flowers which appear in shades of pink, salmon, scarlet and white among others. Strap-like leaves emerge after the flowers have blossomed.

Temperature: 70 degrees; 60 degrees when flowering begins.

Light: Shade; Partial sun when blooming.

Water: Very little water until bulb appears, then keep soil moist.

Humidity: Normal level.

Pinching and Pruning: Do not pinch or prune until bulb receeds.

Fertilizer: Every two weeks while blooming.

Soil Contents: Common indoor all-purpose mix.

Propagation: Remove and plant offset bulbs after flowering period is over. You may also try to divide the plant during this period.

Pests and Diseases: Rarely bothered.

Care Rating: **

PELARGONIUM

Common Names: Geranium.

Description: Easy to care for, year round houseplants which bloom in colors ranging throughout the reds, pinks, whites, and purples.

Temperature: 70 degrees day; 60 degrees night.

Light: Direct sun.

Water: Allow the top of the soil to dry out between very thorough waterings/drenchings.

Humidity: Low humidity level.

Pinching and Pruning: Pinch and prune in autumn to keep the plant bushy. Always remove dead flowers and leaves immediately.

Fertilizer: Every two weeks with a fertilizer which is low in nitrogen.

Soil Contents: Common indoor all-purpose mix.

Propagation: Seeds; stem cuttings can be rooted in vermiculite.

Pests and Diseases: Mealybugs, Spider Mites, and Powdery Mildew.

Care Rating: ****

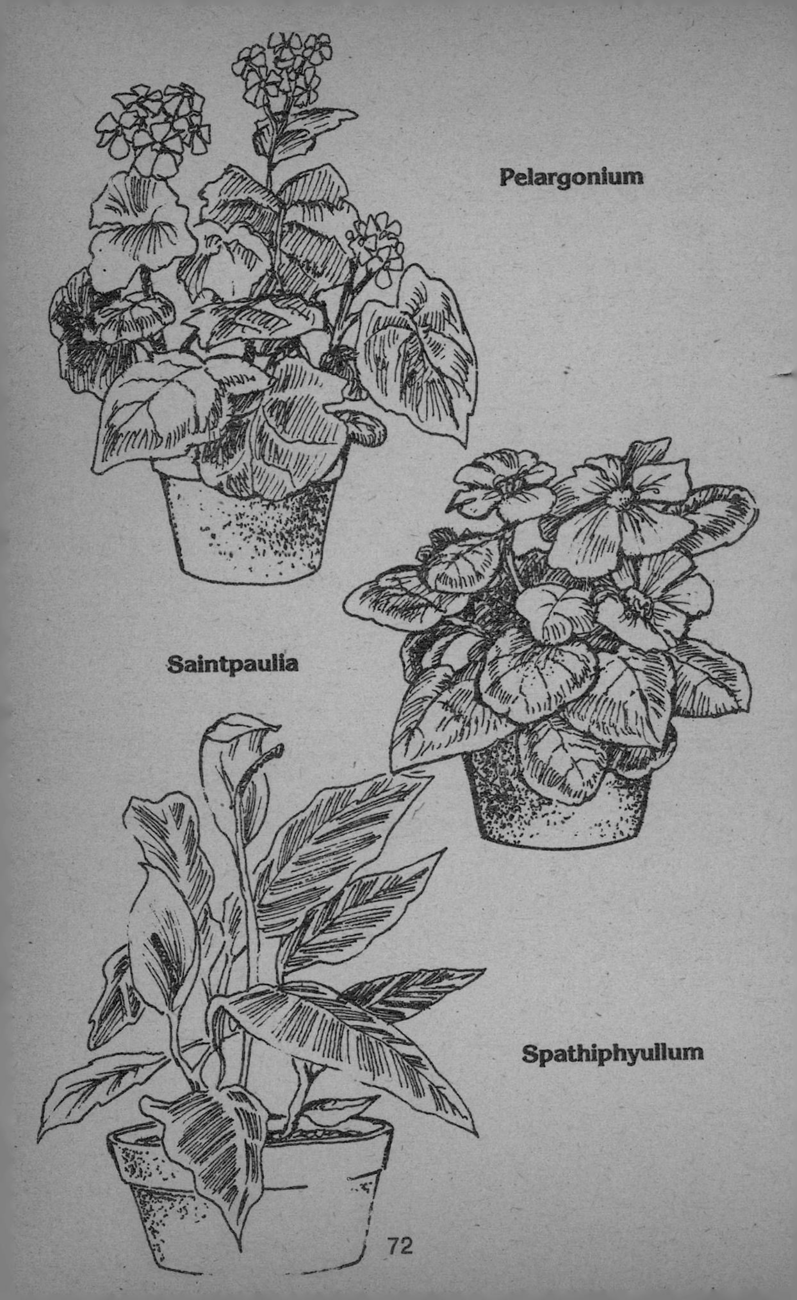
Pelargonium
Saintpaulia
Spathiphyullum

SAINTPAULIA

Common Names: African violet.

Description: The most popular flowering houseplant of modern times, the African violet is a stemless plant with velvety leaves and violet flowers.

Temperature: 75 degrees day; 65 degrees night.

Light: Partial sun in winter; Bright light in summer.

Water: Keep soil evenly moist and only water with lukewarm water. Never allow water to touch the leaves.

Humidity: High level.

Pinching and Pruning: Prune side shoots and always remove dead flowers and leaves immediately.

Fertilizer: Once a month.

Soil Contents: African violet mix.

Propagation: Leaf and stem cuttings, seeds.

Pests and Diseases: Crown Rot, Botrytis Grey Mold, Aphids, Scale.

Care Rating: ****

SPATHIPHYULLUM

Common Names: Peace lily, White flag, Spathe flower.

Description: Long, oval leaves and usually just one or two pure, white sheaths covering flower stalks.

Temperature: 65 to 70 degrees.

Light: Filtered light or Shade.

Water: Keep the soil moist in spring and summer; allow the top of the soil to dry out in between waterings during fall and winter.

Humidity: High level.

Pinching and Pruning: None needed.

Fertilizer: Once a month during growth period.

Soil Contents: Common indoor all-purpose mix. Add sphagnum if necessary.

Propagation: Division.

Pests and Diseases: Scale, Spider Mites.

Care Rating: ****

ORCHIDS

CATTLEYA

Common Names: Cattleya.

Description: These are the most popular group of Orchids, known for their use in corsages. Their flowers bloom in many beautiful and varied colors, including purple, white, lavender, yellow, green and red.

Temperature: 70 degrees day; 60 degrees night.

Light: Partial sun.

Water: Allow the top of the soil to dry out between thorough waterings.

Humidity: High level.

Pinching and Pruning: None needed.

Fertilizer: Use fertilizer formulated especially for Orchids every two weeks during growth period.

Soil Contents: Fir bark.

Propagation: Division.

Pests and Diseases: Leaf Spot, Scale, Spider Mites.

Care Rating: ***

Cattleya

COELOGYNE

Common Names: Coelogyne.

Description: An epiphytic Orchid with spoon-shaped leaves. Its flowers usually appear in light shades of brown (i.e. beige or cream).

Temperature: 65 degrees day; 55 degrees night.

Light: Shade.

Water: Keep soil extremely moist during growth period.

Humidity: High level.

Pinching and Pruning: None needed.

Fertilizer: Use fertilizer formulated especially for Orchids every two weeks during growth period.

Soil Contents: Fir bark.

Propagation: Division.

Pests and Diseases: Leaf Spot, Mealybugs.

Care Rating: **

CYMBIDIUM

Common Names: Cymbidium.

Description: A terrestrial Orchid known for its unusually lengthy blooming period. Foliage is a lovely yellow-green color.

Temperature: 60 degrees day; 50 degrees night.

Light: Filtered light.

Water: Keep soil evenly moist.

Humidity: High level.

Pinching and Pruning: None needed.

Fertilizer: Use fertilizer formulated especially for Orchids every two weeks during winter and spring, and every month during summer and fall.

Soil Contents: Cymbidium Orchid Mix.

Propagation: Division.

Pests and Diseases: Leaf Spot, Scale.

Care Rating: ***

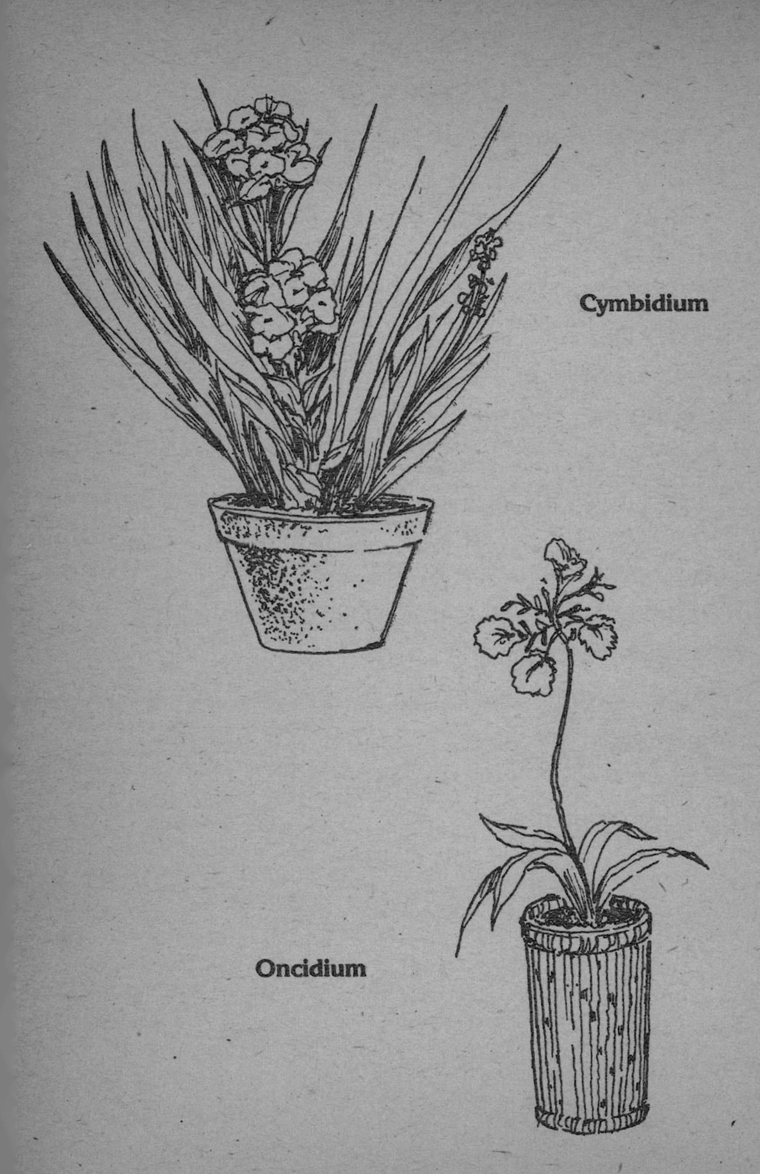
Cymbidium
Oncidium

ONCIDIUM

Common Names: Dancing lady orchid.

Description: A group of epiphytic Orchids known for their stalks of yellow flowers which are dotted with specks of brown.

Temperature: 70 degrees day; 60 degrees night.

Light: Partial sun.

Water: Keep soil evenly moist, allowing the top of it to dry out in between waterings after a growth period.

Humidity: High level.

Pinching and Pruning: None needed.

Fertilizer: Use fertilizer formulated especially for Orchids every two weeks during growth period.

Soil Contents: Fir bark.

Propagation: Division.

Pests and Diseases: Leaf Spot, Scale, Spider Mites.

Care Rating: ***

PAPHIOPEDILUM

Common Names: Lady slipper orchid.

Description: A terrestrial Orchid which produces curved foliage and fragrant flowers which appear to be extremely waxy.

Temperature: 70 degrees day; 60 degrees night.

Light: Bright light.

Water: Keep soil evenly moist throughout the year.

Humidity: Normal level.

Pinching and Pruning: None needed.

Fertilizer: None needed.

Soil Contents: Osmunda Fiber Mix.

Propagation: Division.

Pests and Diseases: Leaf Spot, Spider Mites.

Care Rating: ***

Paphiopedilum

Phalaenopsis

PHALAENOPSIS

Common Names: Moth orchid.

Description: A member of the epiphytes, this Orchid features large, moth-like, multi-colored flowers.

Temperature: 75 degrees day; 65 degrees night.

Light: Filtered light.

Water: Keep soil evenly moist throughout the year.

Humidity: High level.

Pinching and Pruning: None needed.

Fertilizer: None needed.

Soil Contents: Osmunda Fiber Mix.

Propagation: Division.

Pests and Diseases: Leaf Spot, Scale.

Care Rating: ***

FOLIAGE HOUSEPLANTS

ARAUCARIA HETEROPHYLLA

Common Names: Norfolk island pine.

Description: This is a straight tree with symmetrical branches and needlelike foliage. The tree grows very slowly, but can eventually reach a height of ten feet.

Temperature: 60 degrees.

Light: Bright light.

Water: Allow the top of the soil to dry out between thorough waterings/drenchings.

Humidity: Low level.

Pinching and Pruning: None needed.

Fertilizer: Once a year.

Soil Contents: Common indoor all-purpose mix.

Propagation: Very difficult, although you can try using leader cuttings.

Pests and Diseases: Stem or Root Rot.

Care Rating: ****

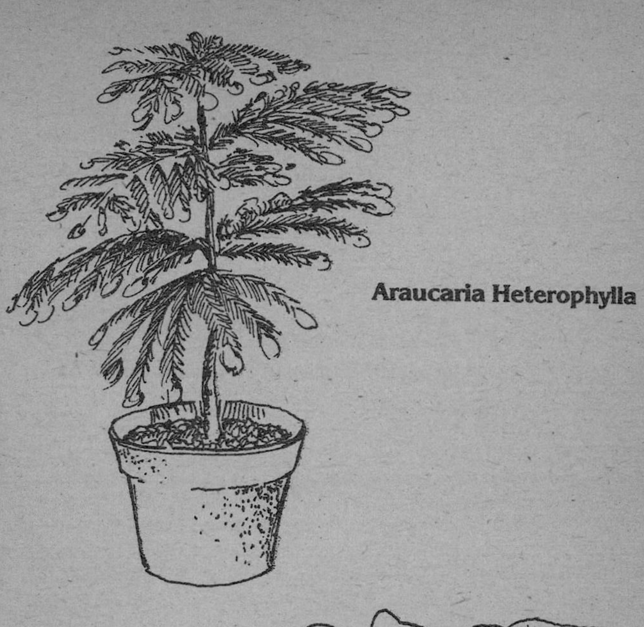

Araucaria Heterophylla

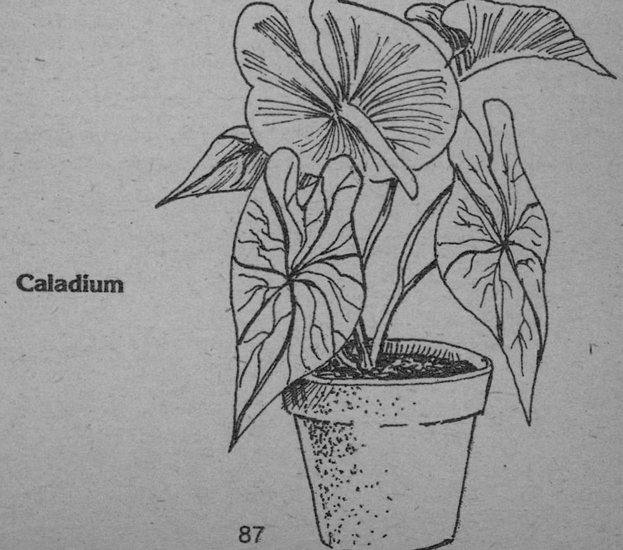

Caladium

CALADIUM

Common Names: Caladium.

Description: Caladium are famous for their extraordinarily colorful leaves. One to two feet in size, the leaves can be green, red, yellow or pink.

Temperature: 75 degrees.

Light: Bright light.

Water: Water frequently during growth period, but allow the top of the soil to dry out completely during dormant season.

Humidity: High level.

Pinching and Pruning: Trim off faded leaves and cut off any dead foliage regularly.

Fertilizer: Fertilize every two weeks during growth period.

Soil Contents: Common indoor all-purpose mix.

Propagation: Seeds, tubers. For tubers, remove them from the container when the plant dries out and place them in peat moss in a cool location until spring approaches. Then divide the tubers and place in small pots in a warm, moist area.

Pests and Diseases: Rarely bothered.

Care Rating: *

CHLOROPHYTUM

Common Names: Spider plant.

Description: Features long, thin green and white leaves. "Baby" plants spring up from the ends of the mother plant's stems.

Temperature: 65 to 75 degrees.

Light: Bright light.

Water: Keep soil evenly moist at all times.

Humidity: Normal level.

Pinching and Pruning: Rotate plant regularly.

Fertilizer: Every two weeks.

Soil Contents: Common indoor all-purpose mix.

Propagation: Division, plantlets. For plantlets, simply cut them off and root in water or peat moss.

Pests and Diseases: Scale, Salt Damage.

Care Rating: ****

Chlorophytum
Dieffenbachia
Coleus

COLEUS

Common Names: Flame nettle, Painted leaf plant.

Description: Velvety leaves with many different colors mark this popular plant. The leaves are often scalloped, and small blue or white flowers sometimes form in autumn.

Temperature: 70 degrees.

Light: Bright light.

Water: Keep soil evenly moist throughout the year.

Humidity: High level.

Pinching and Pruning: Pinch off flowers and growing tips regularly to prevent leggy growth.

Fertilizer: Fertilize every two weeks.

Soil Contents: Common indoor all-purpose mix.

Propagation: Stem cuttings, seeds.

Pests and Diseases: Mealybugs, White Flies.

Care Rating: ****

DIEFFENBACHIA

Common Names: Dumb cane.

Description: A popular houseplant possessing large, speckled green and cream colored leaves. The sap from the canelike stems, if eaten, can result in paralysis of the vocal cords.

Temperature: 65 to 75 degrees.

Light: Bright light.

Water: Allow the top of the soil to dry out completely between waterings.

Humidity: Normal level.

Pinching and Pruning: Remove dead foliage immediately and keep leaves free of dust.

Fertilizer: Fertilize every two weeks during growth period.

Soil Contents: Common indoor all-purpose mix.

Propagation: Root stems and cuttings in sand.

Pests and Diseases: Rarely bothered.

Care Rating: ****

DIZYGOTHECA

Common Names: False Aralia, Threadleaf.

Description: An elegant looking plant with finger-like, bronze-green leaves. Features a single stem which often reaches up to six feet in height.

Temperature: 65 to 70 degrees.

Light: Bright light.

Water: Allow the top of the soil to dry out between thorough waterings.

Humidity: High level.

Pinching and Pruning: None needed.

Fertilizer: Fertilize monthly except in winter.

Soil Contents: Common indoor all-purpose mix.

Propagation: Cuttings.

Pests and Diseases: Aphids, Mealybugs, Scale.

Care Rating: ***

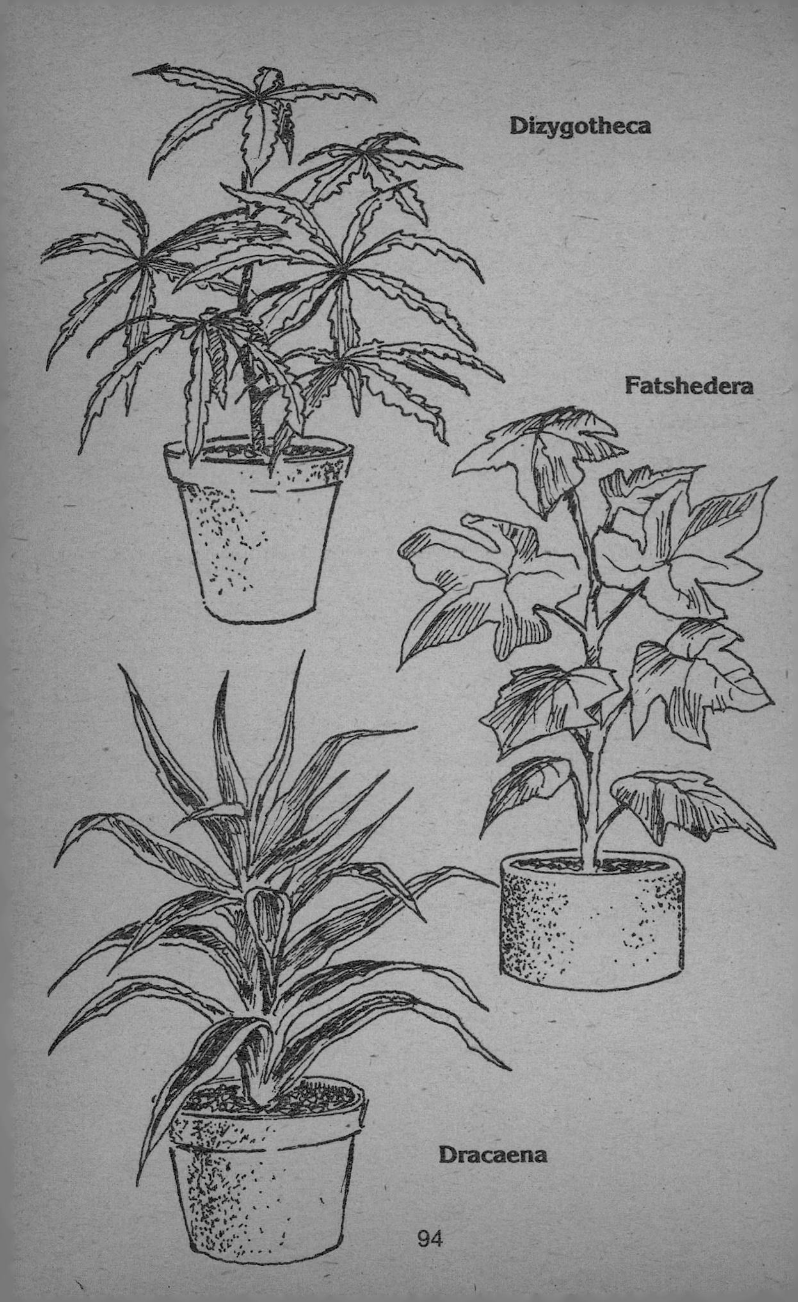
Dizygotheca
Fatshedera
Dracaena

DRACAENA

Common Names: Dragon tree, Cornplant.

Description: A very contemporary tree, Dracaena is a member of the lily family. Its palmlike appearance can be most striking, especially with the taller varieties, which sometimes grow as high as 20 feet tall!

Temperature: 65 to 75 degrees.

Light: Bright light.

Water: Keep soil moist.

Humidity: Normal level.

Pinching and Pruning: Cut off brown tips.

Fertilizer: Fertilize every two weeks during spring and summer.

Soil Contents: Common indoor all-purpose mix.

Propagation: Stem cuttings or top of plant.

Pests and Diseases: Rarely bothered.

Care Rating: ****

FATSHEDERA

Common Names: Tree ivy, Fat lizzie, Botanical wonder.

Description: A very tall plant which resembles overgrown ivy, Fatshedera is actually a hybrid between Fatsia japonica and Hedera helix.

Temperature: 55 to 65 degrees.

Light: Bright light.

Water: Keep very moist at all times.

Humidity: High level.

Pinching and Pruning: Pinch off growth tips and tie branches to a trellis every six months.

Fertilizer: Fertilize monthly during growth period.

Soil Contents: Common indoor all-purpose mix.

Propagation: Root cuttings in water.

Pests and Diseases: Botrytis Grey Mold.

Care Rating: **

FATSIA JAPONICA

Common Names: Japanese aralia.

Description: The leaves of this plant resemble over-sized maple leaves. Waxy, green leaves are sometimes speckled with white.

Temperature: 65 degrees.

Light: Filtered light.

Water: Keep soil evenly moist during growth period, but allow soil to dry out in between waterings during dormant period.

Humidity: Normal level.

Pinching and Pruning: Prune leaves back to the stalk when plant grows unwieldy.

Fertilizer: Fertilize every two weeks except in winter.

Soil Contents: Common indoor all-purpose mix.

Propagation: Seeds, stem cuttings.

Pests and Diseases: Rarely bothered.

Care Rating: ***

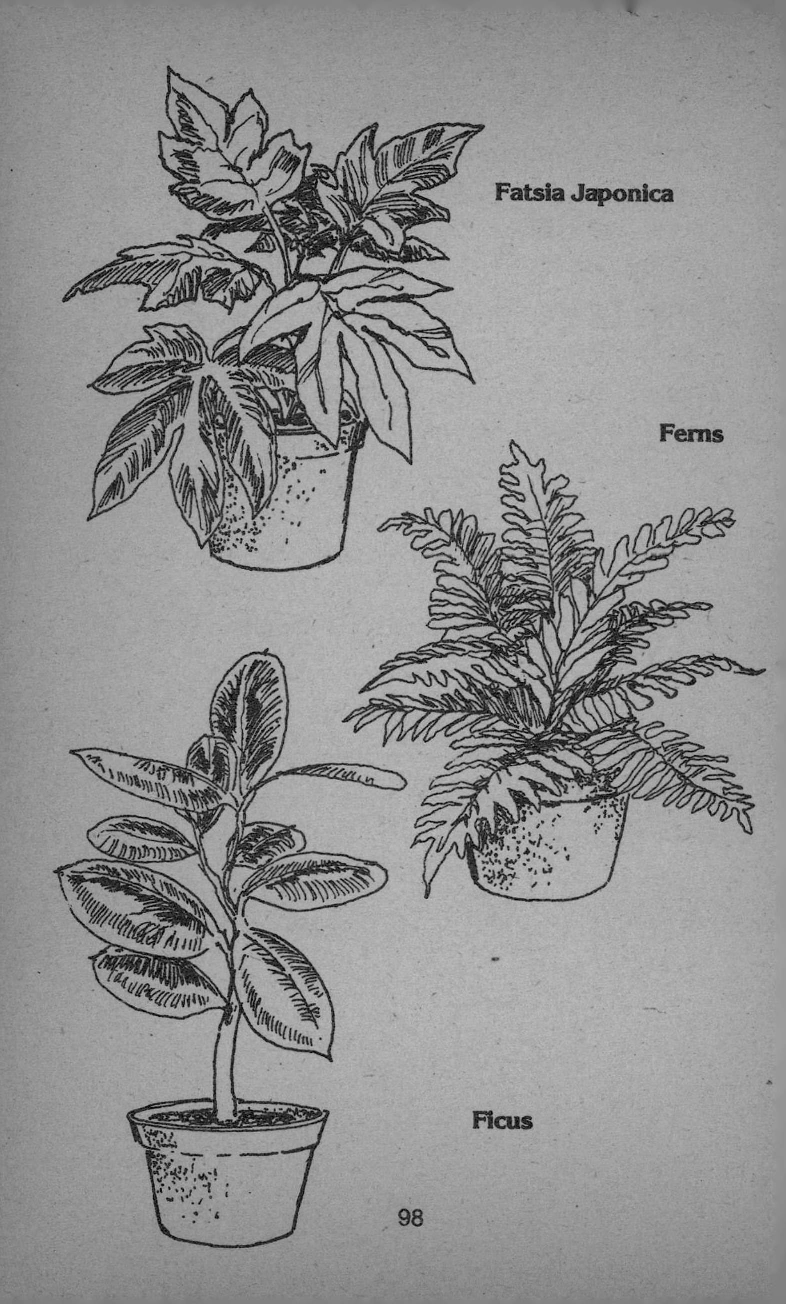
Fatsia Japonica
Ferns
Ficus

FERNS

Common Names: Ferns.

Description: A large group with an interesting and varied history, Ferns have become extremely popular due to their beautiful, delicate foliage.

Temperature: 65 degrees.

Light: Filtered light.

Water: Keep soil evenly moist during summer, but allow the top of the soil to dry out in between thorough waterings in the winter.

Humidity: High level.

Pinching and Pruning: Remove dead leaves and branches immediately.

Fertilizer: Use liquid fertilizer once a month.

Soil Contents: Common indoor all-purpose mix, or Fern Mix.

Propagation: Division.

Pests and Diseases: Scale, Mealybugs.

Care Rating: *

FICUS

Common Names: India rubber plant, Fig.

Description: Ficus is a wide and diverse group of plants whose leaves are marked by a rather stiff, shiny appearance.

Temperature: 65 to 75 degrees.

Light: Bright light.

Water: Allow the top of the soil to dry out between waterings.

Humidity: Normal level.

Pinching and Pruning: Do not allow dust to build up on leaves.

Fertilizer: Every two weeks during spring and summer.

Soil Contents: Common indoor all-purpose mix.

Propagation: Stem cuttings.

Pests and Diseases: Rarely bothered.

Care Rating: ****

HEDERA HELIX

Common Names: English ivy.

Description: This is the best known ivy, with its dark green, trailing or climbing vines. Its leaves are often shiny and leather-like.

Temperature: 60 to 65 degrees.

Light: Partial sun in winter; Bright light in summer.

Water: Keep soil evenly moist throughout the year.

Humidity: High level.

Pinching and Pruning: Prune for a bushier look.

Fertilizer: Fertilize every two weeks during growth period, every month in the winter.

Soil Contents: Common indoor all-purpose mix.

Propagation: Stem cuttings.

Pests and Diseases: Spider Mites, Aphids, Browning Leaf Tips.

Care Rating: ***

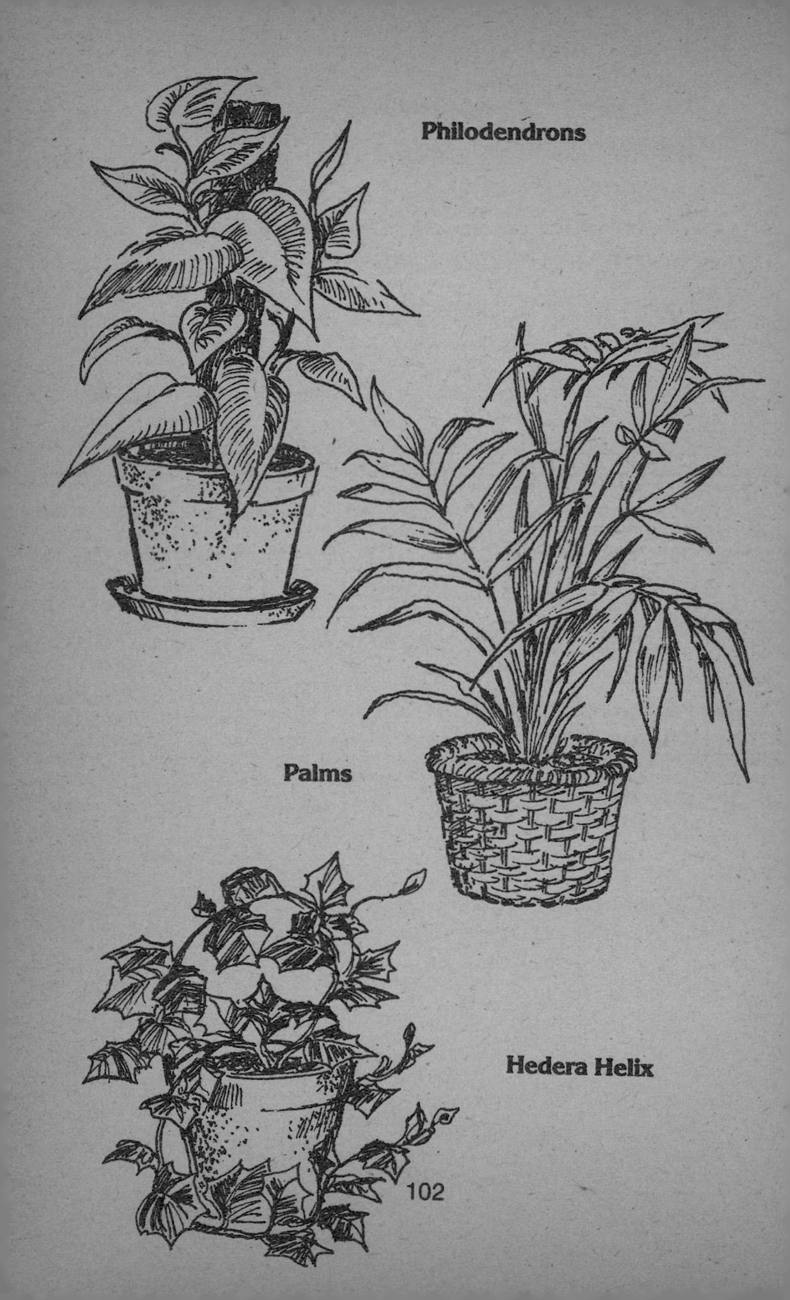
Philodendrons
Palms
Hedera Helix

PALMS

Common Names: Palm.

Description: Palms have been a favorite houseplant for decades. Their lyrical shape and lush greenery add an exotic touch to any decor.

Temperature: 70 degrees.

Light: Filtered light.

Water: Water frequently and thoroughly in summer; in winter allow the top of the soil to dry out between waterings.

Humidity: High level.

Pinching and Pruning: Only prune dead branches.

Fertilizer: Every two weeks except in winter.

Soil Contents: Common indoor all-purpose mix; or add garden loam if desired.

Propagation: Seeds.

Pests and Diseases: Scale, Spider Mites.

Care Rating:****

PHILODENDRONS

Common Names: Philodendron.

Description: The leathery, shiny leaves of these plants appear in many interesting shapes and designs. Because of their attractive look, and because of their ease of care, Philodendrons are found in the majority of houseplant collections.

Temperature: 65 to 75 degrees.

Light: Filtered light.

Water: Keep the soil evenly moist and water thoroughly.

Humidity: High level.

Pinching and Pruning: Wash leaves regularly.

Fertilizer: Use a liquid fertilizer once a month during growth period.

Soil Contents: Common indoor all-purpose mix.

Propagation: Root cuttings in water.

Pests and Diseases: Aphids, Mealybugs.

Care Rating:****

PILEA

Common Names: Aluminum plant.

Description: An unusual plant featuring green leaves with silver stripes. Pilea grow very quickly.

Temperature: 65 to 75 degrees.

Light: Bright light in winter; Filtered light in summer.

Water: Allow the top of the soil to dry out between very thorough waterings.

Humidity: Normal level.

Pinching and Pruning: Pinch back stems frequently.

Fertilizer: Fertilize once a month during the summer.

Soil Contents: Common indoor all-purpose mix.

Propagation: Root cuttings in sand.

Pests and Diseases: Rarely bothered.

Care Rating: ****

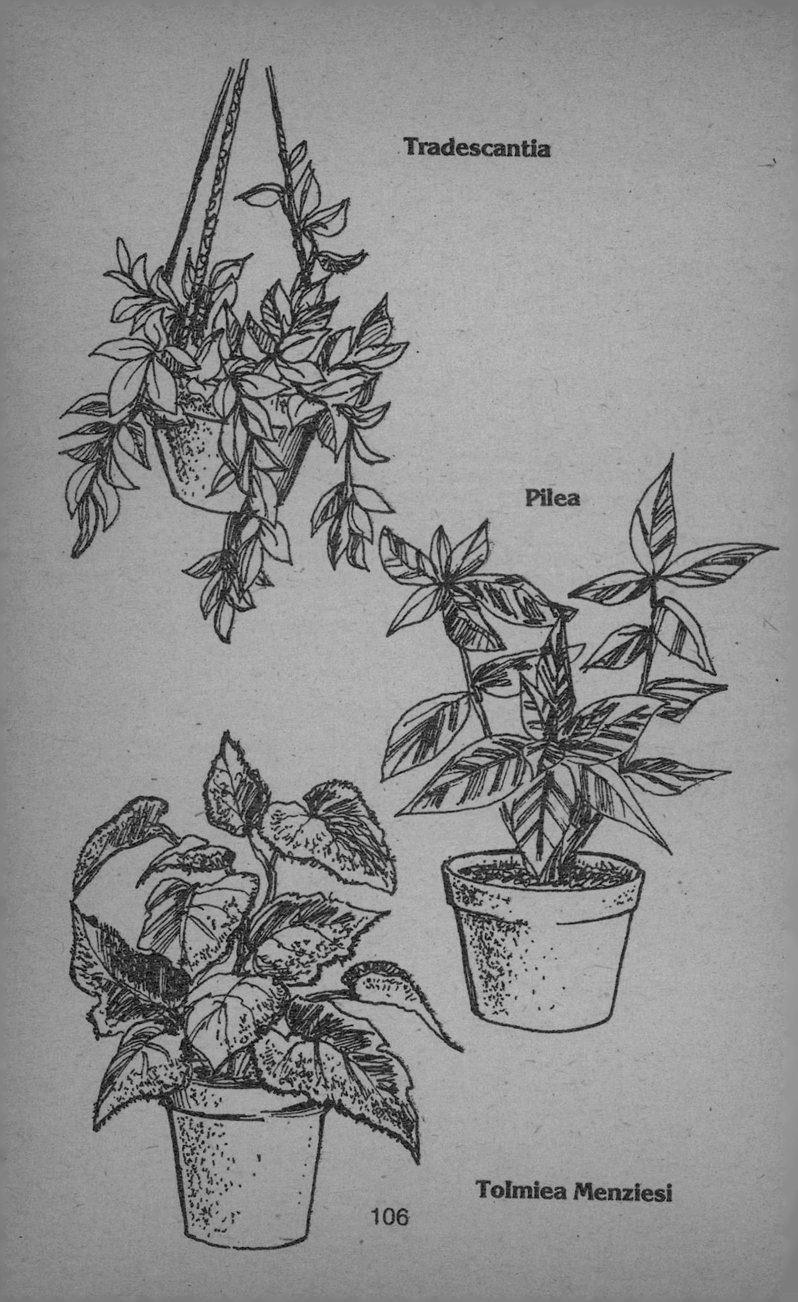
Tradescantia
Pilea
Tolmiea Menziesi

TOLMIEA MENZIESI

Common Names: Piggyback plant, Mother-of-thousands.

Description: A fascinating plant featuring fuzzy, bright green, maple-shaped leaves. New plantlets grow at the base of the leaf and stem of older leaves.

Temperature: 60 to 70 degrees days; 45 to 55 degrees night.

Light: Bright light.

Water: Keep soil evenly moist throughout the year.

Humidity: Normal level.

Pinching and Pruning: Prune to any shape desired and always pinch off dead leaves immediately.

Fertilizer: Fertilize four times a year.

Soil Contents: Common indoor all-purpose mix.

Propagation: Root plantlets in potting soil.

Pests and Diseases: Spider Mites.

Care Rating: ***

TRADESCANTIA

Common Names: Wandering Jew, Inch plant, Chain plant.

Description: Trailing green and white leaves make these plants a natural for hanging baskets. Often times the undersides of the leaves will be fuzzy and purple.

Temperature: 65 to 75 degrees.

Light: Bright light.

Water: Keep soil evenly moist with thorough waterings.

Humidity: Normal level.

Pinching and Pruning: Pinch back for a bushier look.

Fertilizer: Fertilize once a month except in winter.

Soil Contents: Common indoor all-purpose mix.

Propagation: Division or root cuttings in water.

Pests and Diseases: Rarely bothered.

Care Rating: ****

CACTI

CEPHALOCEREUS

Common Names: Old man cactus.

Description: This is a cylindrical cactus, known for its slow, yet tall growth, at times to a height of ten feet. Soft, white bristles — a few inches in length — cover the cactus, and rose colored flowers will appear on its upper portions.

Temperature: 65 to 80 degrees days and nights; 50 to 55 degrees winter.

Light: Direct sun.

Water: Allow soil to dry out between thorough drenchings. Water sparingly in winter.

Humidity: Low level.

Pinching and Pruning: Brush matted hairs with a toothbrush and soapy water.

Fertilizer: Fertilize once every other month.

Soil Contents: Cactus Mix or a soil made up of one part sand, one part garden soil, one half part crushed brick or clay pot, and one half part decayed leaf mold.

Propagation: Seed, division, cuttings.

Pests and Diseases: Root or Stem Rot.

Care Rating: ****

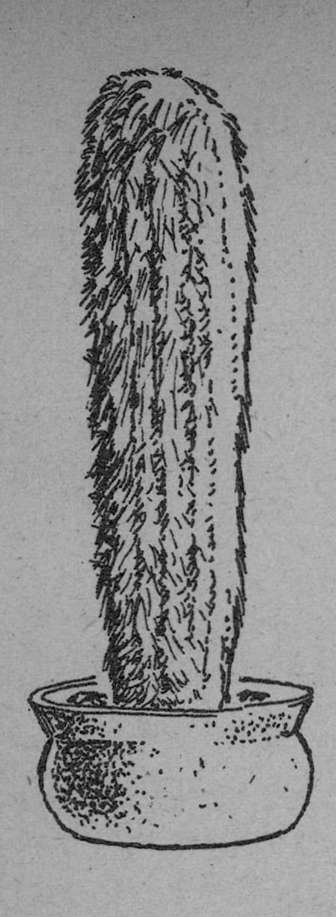

Cephalocereus

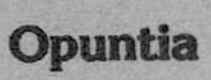

OPUNTIA

Common Names: Prickly Pears, Bunny Ears, Beaver Tails.

Description: This cactus appears with either cylindrical or flat stems. Small batches of spines form bizarre patterns all over the plant's surface.

Temperature: 65 to 80 degrees days and nights; 50 to 55 degrees winter.

Light: Direct sun.

Water: Allow soil to dry out between thorough drenchings. Water sparingly in winter.

Humidity: Low level.

Pinching and Pruning: None needed.

Fertilizer: Fertilize every other month.

Soil Contents: Cactus Mix or a soil made up of one part sand, one part garden soil, one half part crushed brick or clay pot, and one half part decayed leaf mold.

Propagation: Seeds, Cuttings, Pads.

Pests and Diseases: Rarely bothered.

Care Rating: ****

SUCCULENTS

AGAVE

Common Names: Century Plant.

Description: Fleshy, strap-shaped, triangular leaves with sharp edges mark this succulent. The plant dies after flowering, which often takes up to 20 years.

Temperature: 65 to 80 degrees.

Light: Partial sun.

Water: Allow top of soil to dry out between thorough drenchings. In winter water enough to prevent all of the soil from becoming completely dry.

Humidity: Low level.

Pinching and Pruning: None needed.

Fertilizer: Fertilize every month during growth period.

Soil Contents: Common indoor all-purpose mix or Cactus Mix.

Propagation: Seeds, Cuttings, Offshoots. Apply a fungicide to the exposed area of cuttings or offshoots and let dry until healed. Then plant in a fairly dry soil.

Pests and Diseases: Leaf Spot; Root or Stem Rot.

Care Rating: ****

Agave

Aloe

ALOE

Common Names: Aloe.

Description: Aloe is a huge and diverse group of succulents. They are often recognized by their lightly colored flowers and/or tapered leaves. Aloe vera can be used for medicinal purposes.

Temperature: 65 to 80 degrees.

Light: Partial sun.

Water: Allow top of soil to dry out between thorough drenchings. In winter water enough to prevent all of the soil from drying out.

Humidity: Low level.

Pinching and Pruning: None needed.

Fertilizer: Once a month during growth period.

Soil Contents: Common indoor all-purpose soil or Cactus Mix.

Propagation: Cuttings, offshoots.

Pests and Diseases: Leaf Spot; Root or Stem Rot.

Care Rating: ****

CRASSULA

Common Names: Jade plant, Chinese rubber plant.

Description: Crassula features short, flat, fleshy leaves piled up on top of one another. Often times the green leaves appear with bits of red mixed in.

Temperature: 65 to 80 degrees.

Light: Bright light.

Water: Allow top of soil to become dry in between thorough drenchings. In winter, water enough to prevent all of the soil from drying out completely.

Humidity: Low level.

Pinching and Pruning: None needed.

Fertilizer: Fertilize every two weeks during growth period.

Soil Contents: Common indoor all-purpose mix or Cactus Mix.

Propagation: Cuttings.

Pests and Diseases: Leaf Spot, Root or Stem Rot.

Care Rating: ****

Crassula

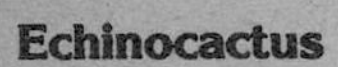

Echinocactus

ECHINOCACTUS

Common Names: Golden barrel.

Description: A cactus shaped like a globe, Echinocactus features long, gold-colored spines. Yellow flowers appear around its top like a crown.

Temperature: 65 to 80 degrees days and nights; 50 to 55 degrees winter.

Light: Direct sun.

Water: Allow the top of the soil to dry out between thorough drenchings. Water sparingly in winter.

Humidity: Low level.

Pinching and Pruning: None needed.

Fertilizer: Fertilize once every other month.

Soil Contents: Cactus Mix or a soil made up of one part sand, one part garden soil, one half part crushed brick or clay pot, and one half part decayed leaf mold.

Propagation: Seeds.

Pests and Diseases: Rarely bothered.

Care Rating: ****

ECHINOPSIS

Common Names: Easter lily cactus.

Description: Large red, white or pink flowers resembling a trumpet mark this unusual cactus. Normally the flowers only bloom at night.

Temperature: 65 to 80 degrees days and nights; 50 to 55 degrees winter.

Light: Direct or Partial Sun.

Water: Keep soil evenly moist. Allow the top of the soil to dry out between waterings during winter.

Humidity: Low level.

Pinching and Pruning: None needed.

Fertilizer: Fertilize once a month.

Soil Contents: Two parts sand, two parts peat moss, and one part leaf mold.

Propagation: Seeds.

Pests and Diseases: Rarely bothered.

Care Rating: ****

Echinopsis

Gymncalycium

GYMNCALYCIUM

Common Names: Spider cactus, Chin cactus.

Description: This is a globular cactus whose ten inch stems sometimes grow in clusters. White, rose, and occasionally yellow flowers blossom in spring and summer.

Temperature: 65 to 80 degrees.

Light: Bright light.

Water: Allow the top of the soil to dry out between thorough drenchings.

Humidity: Low level.

Pinching and Pruning: None needed.

Fertilizer: Fertilize every other month.

Soil Contents: Cactus Mix or a soil made up of one part sand, one part garden soil, one half part crushed brick or clay pot, and one half part decayed leaf mold.

Propagation: Seeds.

Pests and Diseases: Rarely bothered.

Care Rating: ****

MAMMILLARIA

Common Names: Pin cushion cactus.

Description: A popular and diverse group of cacti, mammillaria is noted for its beautiful flowers which bloom in a circle around the top of the cactus.

Temperature: 65 to 80 degrees days and nights; 50 to 55 degrees winter.

Light: Partial sun.

Water: Allow soil to dry out between thorough drenchings. Water sparingly in winter.

Humidity: Low level.

Pinching and Pruning: None needed.

Fertilizer: Fertilize every other month.

Soil Contents: Cactus Mix or a soil made up of one part sand, one part garden soil, one half part crushed brick or clay pot, and one half part decayed leaf mold.

Propagation: Seeds, Cuttings.

Pests and Diseases: Rarely bothered.

Care Rating: ****

Mammillaria
Echeveria

ECHEVERIA

Common Names: Painted lady, Hen and chicks.

Description: Echeverias are noted for their rosette shape and diverse leaf coloring. Yellow, orange and pink flowers also make this one of the more attractive succulents.

Temperature: 65 to 80 degrees.

Light: Direct sun.

Water: Allow top of soil to dry out between thorough drenchings. In winter, water enough to prevent all of the soil from drying out completely.

Humidity: Low level.

Pinching and Pruning: Prune off stems to prevent leggy growth.

Fertilizer: Every two weeks during growth period.

Soil Contents: Cactus Mix or a soil made up of one part sand, one part garden soil, one half part crushed brick or clay pot, and one half part decayed leaf mold.

Propagation: Leaf Cuttings, offshoots. For Leaf Cuttings, be sure to include the dormant bud.

Pests and Diseases: Leaf Spot, Root or Stem Rot.

Care Rating: ****

EUPHORBIA

Common Names: Spurge, Big horned euphorbia.

Description: The Poinsettia is a member of this group of succulents. Usually features many small thorns, interesting textures and colors, and a milky sap that can be poisonous.

Temperature: 65 to 80 degrees.

Light: Partial sun.

Water: Allow the top of the soil to dry out between thorough drenchings. In winter, water enough to prevent all of soil from drying out completely.

Humidity: Low level.

Pinching and Pruning: None needed.

Fertilizer: Fertilize once a month during growth period.

Soil Contents: Common indoor all-purpose mix or Cactus Mix.

Propagation: Cuttings. Use a fungicide on exposed area, let dry and plant in sand.

Pests and Diseases: Leaf Spot; Root or Stem Rot.

Care Rating: ****

Euphorbia

Kalanchoe

KALANCHOE

Common Names: Kalanchoe.

Description: An extremely popular houseplant, Kalanchoes are loved both for their beautiful foliage and their attractive flowers. Makes a wonderful gift plant!

Temperature: 65 to 80 degrees.

Light: Direct sun.

Water: Allow top of soil to dry out between waterings. In winter, water enough to prevent all of soil from drying out completely.

Humidity: Low level.

Pinching and Pruning: None needed.

Fertilizer: Fertilize once a month during growth period.

Soil Contents: Common indoor all-purpose mix or Cactus Mix.

Propagation: Seeds, cuttings.

Pests and Diseases: Leaf Spot; Root or Stem Rot.

Care Rating: ****